Things To Make and Do for
CHRISTMAS

Things To Make and Do for
CHRISTMAS

by Ellen Weiss

A Things to Make and Do Book

Franklin Watts

New York/London/Toronto/Sydney
1980

to Ken R. Deer
and all my deer friends

Library of Congress Cataloging in Publication Data

Weiss, Ellen.
  Things to make and do for Christmas.

  (A Things to make and do book)
  SUMMARY: Christmas projects include directions for making cards, games, decorations, and things to eat.
  1. Christmas decorations — Juvenile literature.
2. Christmas cookery — Juvenile literature. 3. Handicraft — Juvenile literature. [1. Christmas decorations. 2. Christmas cookery. 3. Handicraft]
I. Title.
TT900.C4W44   745.59'41   79-23799
ISBN 0-531-02293-5

ISBN 0-531-02145-9 (pbk.)

Did you know that Christmas
is really a birthday celebration?
It is the birthday of Jesus Christ,
who was born almost 2,000 years ago.
We do not know the exact day that
Christ was born, but we celebrate
Christmas on December 25 every year.

We have parties,

decorate our homes
and Christmas trees,

sing songs,

eat lots of holiday goodies,

and give cards
and gifts to each other.

That's why we are so busy
in our workshop!
You can be busy, too.
Set up a workshop in your house.
Start getting ready about
four weeks before Christmas!

First
Week

Christmas Cards

This is a good time
to make cards to send
to your family and friends!

Make each one different and special!
Here are a few ideas.

Think up your own!

The Teeny Weeny Elf Game

You need:

One person to be the elf
One person to be Santa Claus
At least four other people to play

How to play:

1. The elf sits on a chair in the front
   of the room with his or her back
   to the rest of the players.

2. Santa says to the players:
   "Here's a teeny weeny elf
   Sitting on a little shelf.
   Someone's calling, me oh my!
   Someone's calling _____!"

3. Santa then points to someone in the room. This person changes his or her voice and says, "It is I."

4. The elf has to guess who it is.

5. The elf gets two guesses. If the elf doesn't guess the correct person, he or she has to be the elf again.

If the elf guesses correctly, then the person who changed his or her voice becomes the elf the next time.

Sponge Print Cards

A fast and easy way
to make lots of cards!

You need:

Kitchen sponges
A magic marker
Scissors
Poster paints
A dish
Scrap paper
Construction paper

How to make them:

1. Draw shapes on sponges with a magic marker.

2. Cut the shapes out.
3. Pour some paint in a dish.
4. Dip the sponge shape into the paint.
5. Try printing the shape on scrap paper first.

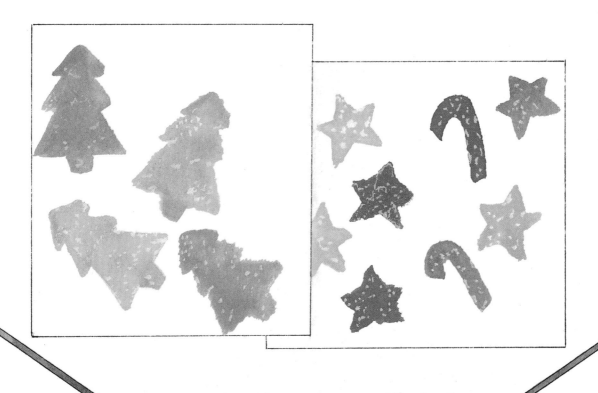

6. Now press the shape onto the front of a folded piece of construction paper.

FOLD

Print the shape a few times on the same card or use different shapes together on one card.

In the 1800s, Christmas trees were called "sugar trees" because of all the sweet things that hung from the branches. On Christmas Day, children shook the trees and gathered as many candies, sweets, and nuts as they could.

How about a
Candy And Nut Holder
for *your* tree!

You need:
A round paper doily
Scotch tape
A pipe cleaner
A stapler
Candy and nuts

How to do it:
1. Fold the doily in half and then in half again.
2. Make a cone shape and tape the cone where it joins.
3. Staple the pipe cleaner on each side to make a handle.
4. Fill the holder with nuts and candy or sweets and hang it on your tree.

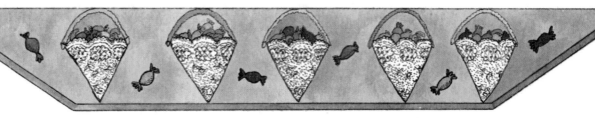

What animal can see just
as well from either end?

A reindeer with its
eyes closed.

"I'm dreaming of a white Christmas."
"Looks like rain, dear."

Second Week

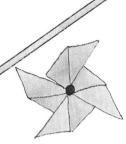

Time to dress up your house for the holidays with a
Pinwheel Wreath

You need:

A pencil	A 10-inch (25-cm) (diameter) plate
A ruler	A 6-inch (15-cm) (diameter) plate
Green construction paper	Thin cardboard
Scissors	Paste
A stapler	Red construction paper
	Red ribbon

How to do it:

1. Draw ten 4-inch (10-cm) squares on the green construction paper and cut them out.

2. Cut each square on the dotted line.

 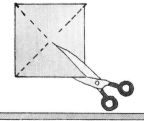

20

3. Fold and staple in the middle.

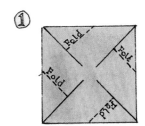  

4. Place the larger plate over a piece of thin cardboard and trace the shape with a pencil.

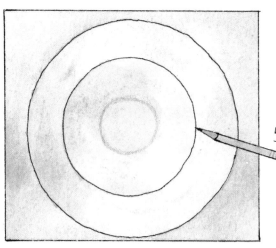

5. Place the smaller plate in the middle of your large circle and trace around it.

6. Cut along the lines you have drawn. Now you have the base for your wreath.

7. Glue each pinwheel onto the base.

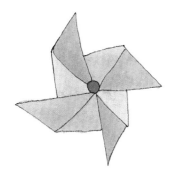

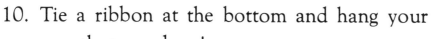

8. Cut ten tiny circles out of the red construction paper. These will be berries.
9. Glue the berries onto the middle of each pinwheel.

10. Tie a ribbon at the bottom and hang your wreath on a door!

Here's a simple treat to make!
Christmas Snow Logs

For three logs,
You need:
A banana
Peanut butter
Shredded coconut
A table knife

How to make them:

1. Cut a banana in three pieces.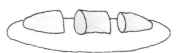

2. Spread peanut butter all over each piece.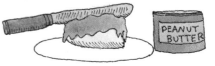

3. Roll the pieces in coconut.

4. Serve.

Hang a
Dancing Santa Ornament
on your tree!

You need:

3 pieces of cardboard,
   each 3 inches (7.6 cm)
   by 4 inches (10 cm)

A pencil
Scissors
A hole puncher
4 paper fasteners

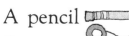

A red magic marker
Red paper
A black magic marker
Cotton (or cotton wool)
Paste
Red yarn

How to do it:

1. Draw Santa's head and body on one piece
   of the cardboard.

2. Draw two arms and two legs on the other
   pieces of cardboard.

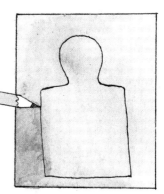

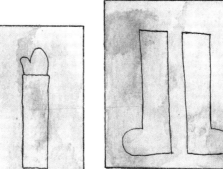

3. Cut all the shapes out.

4. Punch four holes in the body shape.
5. Punch a hole in each leg and in each arm.

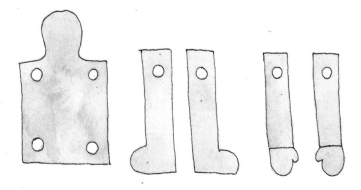

6. Put all the pieces together with paper fasteners. The arms and legs will move.

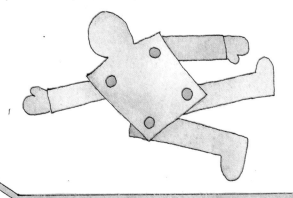

7. Use a red magic marker to make the body red.
8. Now you can decorate Santa:
   Use red paper for his hat.
   Use black magic marker to make black boots.
   Paste cotton for Santa's beard and moustache.
9. Punch a hole in Santa's hat.
10. String yarn through the hole and tie Santa on your Christmas tree.

Can you find the real Santa?

Question:

What's red and white and gives presents to good little fish on Christmas?

Answer:

Sandy Claws

Can you say this tongue twister fast five times?

Snow slows Santa's sled.

Third
Week

Bakers' Clay Ornaments

You need:

A bowl	Tin foil
⅓ cup (80 ml) of water	A sharpened pencil
½ cup (125 ml) of salt	Poster paint
1 cup (250 ml) of flour	Paint brushes
A baking sheet	Shellac or varnish
	Yarn

How to do it:

1. Mix the salt, water, and flour in a bowl with your hands to form the clay.
2. Take bits of the clay and make different shapes.
3. Place each shape on a baking sheet covered with foil.

4. Make a hole at the top of each shape with the point of a pencil.

5. Ask a grown-up to set the oven at 275°F (135°C) and bake for one hour until brown.

6. Let the shapes cool and then paint them.

7. When the paint is dry, coat the shapes with shellac or varnish.

8. String with yarn and hang on your Christmas tree! Or give one to a friend as a gift.

Surprise your friends with
North Pole Cupcake Cones

You need:

Ice cream cones that are flat
  on the bottom
A baking sheet
Any cupcake or cake mix
A bowl
A mixing spoon
Icing
Shredded coconut
Chopped walnuts and raisins

How to do it:

1. Place six ice cream cones on a baking sheet.
2. Make the cake mix according to the instructions and pour the batter in each cone. Leave an inch (2.54 cm) of space at the top.

3. Ask a grown-up to set the oven at 375°F (190.5°C).

4. Place cupcake cones in the oven and bake
   for 20 to 25 minutes.

5. When they are done, let them cool for half an hour.
   Then ice and decorate them with coconut,
   chopped nuts, and raisins. Use your imagination!

6. Serve.

How about printing
Candy Cane Wrapping Paper

You need:

A piece of corrugated cardboard,
   4 inches (10 cm) by 5 inches (12.70 cm)

A pencil

Scissors

A piece of styrofoam (polystyrene),
   4 inches (10 cm) by 5 inches (12.70 cm)

Glue

Red and green tempera paint

A paint brush

White paper

How to do it:

1. Draw a candy cane shape on the cardboard. Be sure you draw the shape from A to B.

2. Cut the shape out. Peel only one side of the cardboard (so that the wavy side shows). Glue it onto the styrofoam.

3. Dip your paint brush into the red paint.
4. Paint the candy cane.
5. Then press the candy cane onto the white paper.

6. Coat the candy cane with paint and print it again.
7. Print the candy cane as many times as you like.

You can even make two candy canes. Paint one red and one green, and then combine them on the paper.

Your gift will look beautiful and special.

Do you know why Christmas trees are always evergreen trees?

The evergreen tree is the "tree of life." It stays green all winter.

Evergreens give us the feeling of hope.

You can grow your own
Mini Christmas Tree!

You need:

A pine cone (the bigger the better)

Water

A small container

Soil

Grass seed

How to do it:

1. Remove the stem of the pine cone so the bottom is flat and the cone will stand up.
2. Soak the pine cone in some water for a few minutes.

3. Remove it from the water.
4. Place it in a container that has half an inch (1.25 cm) of water in it.

5. Sprinkle some soil on the pine cone.
6. Then sprinkle the grass seed evenly over your pine cone.

7. Put it in a sunny spot. Make sure there is always enough water in the container.

8. The grass will grow within two weeks. When it does, trim it with scissors.

Fourth
Week

Seven Layer Cookies

are yummy treats
that everyone will love!

You need:

¼ pound (1 stick) (120 gr) of butter

A baking pan, 9 inches (22.86 cm) by 13 inches (33 cm)

A cup (250 ml) of graham cracker crumbs
  (or any sweet crushed biscuits)

6 ounces (170 gr) of chocolate chips

6 ounces (170 gr) of butterscotch chips

A can of sweetened, condensed milk

A cup (250 ml) of chopped walnuts

Shredded coconut

How to make them:

1. Have a grown-up set the oven at 350°F (177°C).
2. Melt the butter in the baking pan
   in the oven.
3. When the butter is melted, take the pan
   from the oven (butter counts as the first
   layer).

4. Spread the graham cracker or biscuit crumbs evenly over the pan.
5. Spread the chocolate chips on top.
6. Spread the butterscotch chips on top.
7. Spread the condensed milk on top.
8. Spread the coconut.
9. Spread the walnuts.
10. Bake them for 30 to 35 minutes, until they are golden brown.
11. When cool, slice and serve them.

Build a
Christmas Card Cookie House
(to hold your seven-layer cookies)

You need:

A pencil

A ruler

A piece of construction paper,
9 inches (22.86 cm) by
12 inches (30 cm)

7 Christmas cards you got last year
(heavy paper)

Scissors

A hole puncher

Yarn

Tin foil

How to do it:

1. Draw a rectangle, 4½ inches (11.41 cm) by 4 inches (10 cm) on a piece of construction paper.

2. Cut out the rectangle. This will be Pattern 1.

Pattern 1

3. Put Pattern 1 over the front of a Christmas card and trace around it with your pencil. Do this on five Christmas cards.

4. Cut along the lines you have traced.

5. Measure and cut out a rectangle 4½ inches (11.41 cm) wide by 7 inches (17.78 cm) high on construction paper.

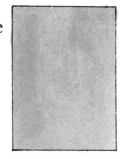

6. Measure halfway up the sides (3½ inches) (8.87 cm) and make a dot on each side. Put a dot in the middle of the 4½ inch (11.41 cm) side.

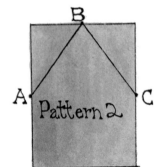

7. Draw a line from Dot A to Dot B. Draw a line from Dot B to Dot C.

8. Cut along lines to form a peak for the roof. This is Pattern 2.

9. Place Pattern 2 on a Christmas card and trace around it. Cut the shape out. Do this twice.

10. Punch holes in all the shapes.

11. Tie shapes together with yarn.
12. Line the inside with foil and fill with your seven-layer cookies.

Play
Find My Sheep
(a guessing and running game)

You need:

One person to be the shepherd
At least five or six other people
(the more the better)

How to play:

1. Ask your friends to sit on the floor in a circle.

2. The shepherd thinks of a person in the circle who will be a lost sheep. The shepherd keeps this a secret.

3. The shepherd walks around the circle and taps
   a player and asks "Have you seen my sheep?"

4. The shepherd describes someone in the circle
   to the person tapped. The shepherd might say:
   "My sheep is wearing a red sweater and blue shoes."
5. The player now tries to guess who the sheep is.
   When he or she makes the correct guess,
   the shepherd says "Yes."

6. Then the guesser chases the sheep around the circle.
7. If the chaser catches the sheep before the sheep
   returns to his or her place, the chaser becomes the
   shepherd. If not, the sheep becomes the shepherd.

You can make a
Paper Peppermint Stick

You need:

A pencil

A piece of white construction paper,
   9 inches (22.86 cm) by 12 inches (30.48 cm)

A ruler

A red crayon

Scissors

Tape

How to do it:

1. Measure a square 9 inches (22.86 cm) by 9 inches (22.86 cm) on a piece of white paper and cut it out.

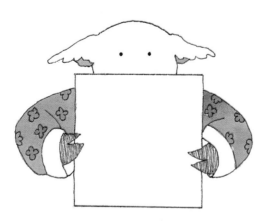

2. Draw lines on the square with a red crayon.

3. Turn the square face down.
4. Roll your paper square from A to B.

5. Tape the end.

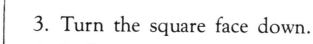

6. Bend and curl one end.
7. Hang on your Christmas tree!

The Peppermint Stick Song

Oh I took a lick on my peppermint stick and it tasted really yum-my, It used to be on my Christmas tree but now it's in my tum-my.

CHORUS

Yo~ho yummy~oh yummy yummy yum-my

Yes it used to be on my Christmas tree but now it's in my tum-my!